The History of Men's Raiment

Also from Westphalia Press
westphaliapress.org

The History of Men's Raiment

by The Edson Lewis Company

WESTPHALIA PRESS
An Imprint of Policy Studies Organization

Westphalia Press
An imprint of Policy Studies Organization
1527 New Hampshire Ave., NW
Washington, D.C. 20036
info@ipsonet.org

ISBN-13: 978-1-63391-540-4
ISBN-10: 1-63391-540-9

Cover design by Jeffrey Barnes:
jbarnesbook.design

Daniel Gutierrez-Sandoval, Executive Director
PSO and Westphalia Press

Updated material and comments on this edition
can be found at the Westphalia Press website:
www.westphaliapress.org

THE HISTORY OF MEN'S RAIMENT

THE HISTORY OF MEN'S RAIMENT

STROUSE & BROTHERS
BALTIMORE MD.

Historical Introduction.

HISTORY cannot tell us of the clothes first worn, though the earliest man is supposed to have daubed his body with colored clays, rather as a decoration than utility, and later adorned his hair with feathers and his back with skins. About 2500 B.C., the Egyptian dressed in a long gown of fine linen, wearing a necklace and finger rings. With the coming of horses, about 858 B.C., the gown became a divided skirt to permit riding astride, really the forerunner of pantaloons; while the Phenicians, great sailors and traders of Medieval days, wearing a tunic and trousers, had reached Britain and given this style to the native. The Briton living in a cold country clung to this costume, though two invasions by the Romans, modified his dress and really started the history of men's raiment.

Following the Roman Invasion comes the Norman Conquest, each influencing the British dress.

The Thirteenth Century was influenced by France, costumes being costly, gracefully draped, rich and simple. The Fourteenth Century was an era of extravagance, such that Parliament regulated a man's dress by act. Gloves became known and the tailor is first spoken of. Colors were popular, and heraldic devices the rage.

These fashions continued into the Fifteenth Century with little change except that the surcoat was worn to permit showing the doublet beneath. The Sixteenth Century was a period of great importance to English dress, Henry VIII and Elizabeth being two of the most gorgeously clad Monarchs England ever knew. Pictures of the day show the ruff which was of Spanish origin like many another picturesque fashion of this time. These styles persist into the Seventeenth Century, while the costumes of the Eighteenth Century, lacking refinement and grace of earlier times, were quaint and picturesque, showing cocked hats, wigs and muffs. Fatherland fashion was now carried into the Colonies in America, where the people, stern and sensible, lived close to nature and dressed accordingly.

The Revolutionary War and severance of allegiance to the Crown, brought independent rule and dress, though men of fashion still looked to the old countries for advice. Years of evolution—difference in thought and natural improvement have led to present day styles, almost a uniform, for they are uniformly worn.

9

ADAM AND EVE.

ROMAN COSTUME 1575 B. C.

Adam and Eve.

The earliest record of the clothing of man comes to us from the Bible, when we are told that the Lord made coats of skins and clothed Adam and Eve. Doubtless this was the only covering used by men for some period. At the time of the heyday of Rome, the ancients could be divided into two great groups, those known as the Trousered and the Untrousered—and the Romans came in the latter class. They had copied their dress from the Greeks, wearing the tunic and the mantle. The Britons, however, dressed like the Gauls in loose fitting tunics, dyed in many colors, and trousers, while in the interior of Britain skins were worn. The Roman invasion, 55 B.C., started the Britons on the road to civilization. Indeed, the new ideas and methods of the Romans were seen manifest in the Briton's dress, and other departments of life. Twice the Romans invaded Britain, giving the natives their costume, and twice the Britons returned to trousers. It is probable that this classic Roman costume was unsuited to the cold British climate, the native dress being warmer and more adapted to conditions. Nevertheless, the classic influence of the Roman dress can be clearly seen in the fashions of England for many centuries.

The Roman Costume, 55 B.C.

Greece and Rome were the great and powerful nations of the northern shores of the Mediterranean. Their costumes were similar. Indeed, they practically set the fashion for that whole section of the world as against that set by the two great branches of the Scythic or Northern Asiatic Family which had overrun Europe, and colonized the southern part of Britain long before the Roman invasion. The Roman dress consisted of a tunic reaching just above the knees, gathered at the waist with a cord; the mantle reached to the ankles, and was fastened on the right shoulder with a round buckle. Senators wore a tunic edged with a purple border, called the Latus Clavus; Knights wore one edged with a narrow border. At the time of the invasion of Britain, the Romans exposed to the rigors of the northern climate, adopted in conjunction with the tunic, tight fitting trousers that reached to the calf of the leg, thus copying the Phenicians, who were at that time the great merchant nation of the Orient, and who had reached all portions of the known world, and even Britain, the Britons having practically adopted their costume prior to 55 B.C.

History of the House of Strouse & Brothers.

THE history of the house of Strouse & Brothers, Baltimore, Maryland, now one of the leading and largest manufacturers of ready-to-wear clothing in the country, reads like the story of the acorn and the oak, for this has been a concern that grew from the very smallest start.

In 1866, Isaac Strouse, a merchant of but limited means, but of most extended ability, unfailing energy and unbounded faith in the future of ready-made clothing, started a little shop, one that was most unpretentious, on Pratt Street, Baltimore. This little plant was devoted to the manufacture of ready-made clothes. It was founded on faith, and how keen the insight, and how capable the business ability and how extended the integrity of the man who started it, we are best able to judge by the organization as it stands to-day, a monument of its kind, surely, a monument to the industry.

It was the aim of the manufacturer to make the product of his shop "just a little better" than the best produced in that day. Not only did he select his goods with judgment, but he manufactured them with unusual care, and the clothes that came from that shop were found so perfect, so enduring, and so satisfactory in every way, that it was to be expected that the business should grow and expand, and grow again, as it certainly did, for within a short time it became

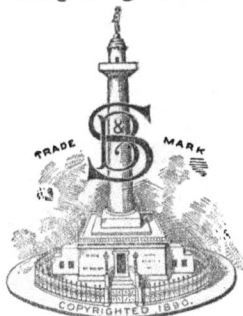

impossible for one director to manage its affairs, hence a new company was organized, that of Strouse & Brothers, composed of the originator of the firm, Isaac Strouse, and his brothers, Leopold, Samuel and Benjamin, assisted also by Samuel Rosenthal, men of the same stamp and of the same untiring energy, cleverness and ability, as the originator.

(*Continued on page* 6)

ANGLO SAXON COSTUME.

TIME OF EDWARD II.

Anglo-Saxon Costume.

This is a period from 436 A.D. to the Norman conquest, 1066. London being a leading commercial center, and England becoming a great maritime nation, nobility began to fashion clothes of the richest stuffs. The conquerors gave the freest rein to their extravagant inclinations, men wore a short tunic tucked into wide breeches which reached to the knees. Under the tunic was a white shirt (indeed, the Saxons are credited with having worn this garment commonly, as early as the Eighth Century) the sleeves of which were tight and wrinkled over the wrist. Upon the legs were loose fitting drawers of natural color, bound around the leg from the ankle to the knees with straps. The better classes wore socks and shoes of skin and leather, shaped to the foot, and buckled across the instep. The coat, semi-circular in shape, fastened over the right shoulder by means of a large, square brooch. The Saxons had a great passion for embroidery, and an extended knowledge of it. The Norman Noble who wished to make a marked difference between his costume and the Britons', wore a mantle, which gave room for much individual taste.

Dress of the Time of Edward II.

This period shows the costume developed to excess, many fripperies being created. Edward II was a monarch of insignificant character, but noted for his luxuriousness. Men of this period wore a hood with a liripipe of great length. They wore new vests called "Cotehardie," striped in angular bars, made of cloth or silk, tight to the body, and close over the hips. The sleeves went to the elbow, and from there, hanging and narrow, showed a sleeve belonging to an undergarment. Around the waist was a plain black belt. From it, hung a triangular pouch. The tights had one leg blue and one leg red, while the shoes were shaped to the foot with great, long pointed toes, so long that at times they were fastened by chains to the knees, or even to the waist, so their wearers might get about. Extravagance in dress led Parliament to regulate material and decoration according to rank. The fashion of wearing and carrying gloves now first found favor. This time saw the introduction of particolored dress, the custom of wearing lappets hanging from the elbows, and the increased popularity of heraldy, servants and retainers being furnished with clothes of the heraldic colors of their masters.

(*Continued from page* 4)

The new organization, in enlarged quarters and with the same skill and determination to make their product all that it should be, carried the business into larger quarters from time to time, until in the year 1893 the firm erected a large and commodious building at the corner of Lombard and Paca Streets, Baltimore, and became its sole occupants.

The new building was dedicated to the manufacture of "High Art Clothing," now trademarked with the famous Washington Monument seal, and known to the best dressers everywhere.

The years following this time have been an era of advancement. Styles have been carefully interpreted, discrimination being used in presenting them to the public, and the continued favor with which the line is accepted, and the fact that it meets with distribution all over the country, is continual evidence of its worth.

In the forty-six years following the organization of the original firm, while no change has occurred in the ideal that created this business, nor in the policy of the house, nor in the abilities that have directed its fortunes, there has, nevertheless, been a change in the personnel of the firm: Two members have since passed away, while the originator himself has retired, leaving future destinies to brother and sons. In the hands of the younger generation, every effort is being made to maintain not only the standard by which "High Art Clothing" is known throughout the land, but the same ideals of business integrity that were created so many years before.

A MAN OF THE TIME OF EDWARD V.

THE ELIZABETHAN PERIOD.

19

A Man of the Time of Edward V (1461).

The influence of the costume of the Fourteenth Century, seems to have extended into that of the Fifteenth Century, some differences occurring toward the end of the century. The most observable change in the costume of the time is the opening of the front of the surcoat, the result being that the doublet beneath could be seen. A man wore a short tunic pleated into large folds above the belt. The sleeves were long, and cut from the shoulder to the waist, where they were sewed together again. Cuff, collar and sleeve openings were edged with fur. The under sleeves were full and of rich silk. His hat was tall, and a long feather was brooched into one side of it. Tights were worn, and the shoes had long pointed toes. At this time, too, it was necessary to check the wearing of excessive apparel, and an act was created making it unlawful except in certain ranks, to wear certain materials or certain colors, though exceptions were made for royal favorites.

The Elizabethan Period.

The Sixteenth Century is one of the most important in English History. Things were done on a magnificent scale and with reckless extravagance. Henry VIII, and Queen Elizabeth, stand out in history as the most gorgeously clad rulers England ever knew. Enthusiasm in dress was the chief consideration of the nobles. Indeed, the men were more extravagant than the women, which was generally true during all of these periods. Colonization existed on a large scale and the maritime energy of England reached colossal proportions. Clothes were of rich satins and velvets of many hues. A man of the period wore a close fitting doublet, the sleeves being very wide and ornamented. The jornet, a loose cloak, worn over the doublet, was without sleeves, allowing the sleeve of the doublet to show. The French breeches were tight, ruffled in puffs about the thighs. The stockings were of silk, and the man most proud of his legs, wore no garters. Shoes were shaped to the foot, and made of various leathers, but the glory of this period was the starched ruff which grew to wonderful proportions, giving a finished touch to the costume already so stiff and padded, that a knight unfortunate enough to drop anything, must call a servant to pick it up for him.

The Dress of 1727.

The Eighteenth Century as a period of dress is somewhat lacking in refinement and grace. Nevertheless, dress of this period is especially quaint and picturesque. The coat and vest of this time were very long, extending to the knees, the former trimmed with embroidery or lace, having large sleeves and very huge cuffs. The waistcoat had full flaps and the cravat was of lace. The shoes had a long tongue showing above bow and buckle, and the stockings were usually white, and the hat black, edged with lace. Pockets, cuffs and buttons commenced to make their appearance as prominent and marked features of the coat. Long flowing wigs were also used during a part time of this century, and the cocked hat, a descendant of the high crowned hats of the reign of Elizabeth, were now appearing. Indeed, this hat still continues the correct headgear for court dress and high rank in army and navy.

The Cavalier. Time of Charles I.

The marvels of the costumes of the Elizabethan period could not be denied a continuation to the following century, though with Charles I came the Cavalier, who wore a broad brim hat with a feather, a Vandyke collar of lace and a doublet of velvet. Each sleeve had a long slash which was filled with bright colored silk, as were the breeches. He wore high heeled riding boots, tight fitting to the knees, but very full at the top. His gauntlet gloves were lined with silk. His sword hung from a broad strap which went over the right shoulder. This period really sees the introduction of knee breeches as a garment generally worn. These were either buttoned at the side or tied about the knees. Padded clothes too, had secured temporary preference, as one of the monarchs of the time, James I, fearful of assassination, looked with great favor upon padded garments as a defence from dirk or stiletto. However, in the day of the Cavalier, the chief object was to appear slim, graceful and elegant. Indeed, the time of the Cavalier can be considered as the best era of grace and tasteful ornamentation in England.

CAVALIER.

MAN OF 1787

COLONIAL 1775.

THE BEAU BRUMMELL

Colonial.

Conditions of strife brought on by differences in political faiths, trouble between church and state, and ill feeling caused by the extravagances of the one class and the frugality of the other, all commenced to reflect in the costumes of the day. Dress in the Colonial period appeals to us as a more rational and possible costume; it was in good taste and very pleasing. A gentleman wore a wig which was formed in a roll over the ears and fastened in the back with a black satin bow, his full skirted coat trimmed with flowered design, opened to show the dainty cravat. The waistcoat was much shorter and elaborately embroidered. The sleeves had large turned back cuffs with lace frills. Breeches were loose and beribboned at the knee. Stockings were of silk and black buckled shoes with red heels completed the costume. The world had now, much more to think of with many new inventions and the tremendous broadening of the times, and dress seemed to have a less serious import, though it was, nevertheless, a matter of moment.

The Beau Brummell. Period of 1820.

This was a period of reform. Not only had the Revolutionary War been fought, its issue in favor of the Colonists having a subduing effect both at home and in the Colonies, but the War of 1812, another conflict with England and her former dependencies, now the United States, had also been fought and similarly decided. Dress became more rational—indeed, quite possible—and we can look upon the fashion of the time of Beau Brummell with much pleasure, for it was picturesque. Here we see the coat slightly altered in our evening dress, having come into fashion in about 1799, and called the "Jean-de-Bry," the vest light colored, also the breeches, which fitted the leg well. White stockings were worn, black shoes with a square buckle, a watch fob, and a cane with an ivory top and hanging tassels, was carried. The hat was light colored and high, the collar high and pointed, and the stock slightly starched. A vogue of the time was side whiskers and the man of that period was, considering the time and what had gone before, most charming.

26

Fashion of the Period of 1860.

Notwithstanding the farewell given by the world to the fripperies of the last centuries—that the world had settled down to the busier times of the modern day, considerable attention was still—as it probably always will be—paid to dress in the Nineteenth Century. But clothes had become more sombre in cut and color. About the time of 1860, the coat worn by men was similar to the present day Prince Albert, the collars and cuffs of which were black velvet. With this coat a light colored vest and trousers were worn, the popular color being light tan. Square toed shoes neither buttoned nor laced, but fitted closely, were pulled on with much difficulty. A very high tiled hat with a small brim was worn, a collar and stock were similar to those of the day of 1825, the stock being black with a bow instead of white with lace, as formerly. The hair was rather long and fell over the ears. It is not difficult to trace the relation of the Continent style upon the style of this modern day. The high silk hat had been worn in England many years before. The Prince Albert was an adoption of an older style as was the stock, and the hair worn long, reminiscent of the days of the wig.

The Period of 1890.

This is a time of comparatively recent issue. In fact, the style of this day is not too remote to be recognized as having a very close relation to the dress of the present time. It is not hard to recall that men wore derby hats high and full in crown, the brim very narrow, the coat of the suit short and rounded away at the bottom, the lapels small and cut very high, no crease in the trousers, and that shoes had a small abrupt square toe. The collar of the time was a modified reproduction of the collar of 1860. A tie had now taken the place of the stock, though the knot was of unusual size. Linked linen cuffs were practically unknown, round ones being worn exclusively, while the gloves that were now in vogue had three black bars stitched on the backs. While this costume was reasonably American, it was, nevertheless, influenced as usual by the styles from the other side.

FASHION OF THE PERIOD OF 1869

PERIOD OF 1890

Policy of the House.

W ITH the inception of the firm of Strouse & Brothers, Baltimore, Md., a fixed and definite policy was created, and in building this immense business, the firm has been guided solely in accordance with these precepts and correct business ethics of the highest character.

This was one of the first concerns to devote themselves exclusively to the making and selling of ready-to-wear clothes of the finest quality, manufacturing solely on a quality basis; that is to say, in accordance with the finest manufacturing details.

Their employees have always been selected from the most capable to be had.

They have always housed their labor in up-to-date, well-lighted, sanitary factories.

Their employees have been brought to a realization of the methods of the firm, and the fact that "High Art Clothing" is ever to be strictly a quality and not a quantity production. Materials fit to associate with this perfect manufacture have been the only ones selected. None has ever been employed that did not measure strictly in accordance with specifications which assured quality.

On the basis outlined above, it has been possible for "High Art Clothing" to be guaranteed, and a guaranty has stood behind every suit ever made by Strouse & Brothers, of Baltimore. Their label is an assurance of the very best material and workmanship throughout.

Twentieth Century "High Art Styles."

"ARUNDEL" AND "THE HOPKINS."

The whole theory of dressing to-day has been reorganized and is accomplished upon a far less involved basis. Dress has almost become a uniform, but we gauge excellence of clothes, or beauty of clothes, or appearance of clothes, by a different scale: They must keep their shape and cut, and wear well—stand the brunt of Twentieth Century service. "High Art Clothing" responds to this demand. Examples of Spring and Summer models for 1912 show the "ARUNDEL" as an exceptionally popular garment, with peaked lapels, made with two buttons. It is a snappy and tasteful style, possesses a seasonable freshness, a thought of Spring, that is bound to appeal to discriminating dressers. However, to strike a responsive note, and to please a different taste, Strouse & Brothers, of Baltimore, have created "The Hopkins," a model that has sedate and sterling qualities that respond to a popular demand. This is a three-button sack. It is devoid of fads or fancies; it possesses elegance and grace that will surely appeal to subdued taste. Both of these models are made in a variety of materials.

"CARVEL" AND "THE ROLAND."

IN olden days, dress of some periods responded to a demand to appear immense and bold of stature, and even to-day there is a survival of this inclination. It is the aim now to look athletic, and Strouse & Brothers, of Baltimore, create the effect differently as exemplified in their "Carvel." This has been designed to give a full and athletic look to the wearer. It is neither gross nor clumsy, rather it is characterized by grace and good form. It is made with three buttons and is about 31 inches long, and its perfect designing creates a very striking appearance. The designers of "High Art Clothing" have given thought to the fitness of things. That is to say, they recognize the appeal of a suitable model for the younger generation and they have adopted certain styles for them, as, for example, "THE ROLAND," which is a typical young men's garment. It is neither freakish nor bold, for while it contains every feature that seasonable fashion demands, it is, nevertheless, refined in appearance and in very good taste.

ARUNDEL   SPRING AND SUMMER 1912   THE HOPKINS

CARVEL   SPRING AND SUMMER 1912   THE ROLAND

Distributors of "High Art Clothing."

IT is fitting that clothes of the character of "High Art Clothing" should be distributed by the most representative dealers in different parts of the country, and Strouse & Brothers, of Baltimore, have been very careful to select those distributors for their products who enjoy the same excellent reputation, who conduct their affairs with the same ideals and business ethics that they themselves maintain. Because of this, not every dealer is a seller of "High Art Clothes," for the mere selling of the clothes themselves does not end Strouse & Brothers' interest in them. They look upon the dealer as an official member of their family. He is their immediate representative to the buyer, and the fact that he sells "High Art Clothing," is evidence that his is the kind of a concern that you would like to deal with, and that you can, with every assurance of confidence and satisfaction.

"High Art Clothing" is sold all over the country, and the leading dealer in every important center carries a full line of these goods, permitting every opportunity for satisfactory selection. Not only that, but he has the facilities for properly fitting the clothes you select, and this is a very important feature. Finally, he is equipped to properly take care of the clothes interests of that large army of users who continually demand the best the market affords, which is synonymous with "High Art Clothing."

Twentieth Century "High Art Styles."

"English No. 2" and "Peabody."

The statement has been made that fashion centers of the world to-day exert a strong influence upon American styles, and it is a fact. Even in the public prints, much is made of the close relation between the styles here and abroad. "English No. 2" represents one of the newest and most graceful of recent creations. It is typical of the season's inclination, soft, rolled front, peaked lapels, slanting pockets and fancy cuffs. It creates an ensemble most fetching and dignified. This is a style that demands the most careful designing and the hand of the master craftsman. Another custom surviving from period days, is the desire to dress in accordance with the very latest fashionable dictates. To this man, the "Peabody" style will especially appeal. This is a nobby model and one that is bound to be popular. It is correct to the last detail and it partakes of the most recent ideas seen in men's dress in all the fashion centers. It has an air of distinction that is most desirable to up-to-date dressers, and notwithstanding its smart cut, it is in good form.

"Norfolk No. 2 and No. 3."

Country life has assumed such great vogue in these days that it has become necessary for dress to adapt itself somewhat to this condition. The season of 1912 will find the Norfolk jacket very fashionable, not only for outing, but for general street wear. The making of a Norfolk jacket requires the skill of the designer and the tailoring of master craftsmen, to make it different from the general run. Excellence in proportion is one of the prime essentials, and character in modeling is another. There is, too, a necessity for discrimination in the selection of material. These combine to create grace in outline, natty appearance and comfort and good form. Norfolk models 2 and 3 combine these features. They are not only handsome and stylish, but distinctly swagger, and in keeping with the spirit of the season for which they are intended. They are made in a number of seasonable materials, and appeal as well to older men as to the younger generation.

NORFOLK No. 2   SPRING AND SUMMER 1912   NORFOLK No. 3

"High Art Styles" for Spring and Summer 1912.

FOR Spring and Summer 1912, "High Art Clothes" are presented in a number of new models, all of them seasonable, yet comfortably so, excellent in appearance and in good form. They are made as usual, in a great variety of materials, such as will receive the stamp of approval from good dressers. Withal, they are made in the inimitable "High Art" fashion, which is assurance of perfection of detail, a guarantee of service and general satisfaction. Men of correct taste in attire, men who appreciate excellent tailoring and fashionable models, will find "High Art Clothing" for Spring and Summer, in accordance with fashion's latest dictates. Nothing either in material or style that is at all startling or freakish is found in "High Art Clothes," though novelties that are graceful and pleasing, such as the up-to-date or nobby dresser appreciates, are shown.

An effort has been made to create in the various models an appeal to the different tastes of men in the different walks of life, and both for young men and their older and more sedate brothers. Considerable latitude will be found to exist in the question of price, irrespective of which, however, the clothes are made as all "High Art Clothing" is—perfectly.

FROM our imprint on the back cover of this booklet, you will note that we are the sponsors for "High Art Clothing" in this vicinity, and it will afford us much pleasure to have you look over the Spring and Summer models for the year 1912. These are advanced styles for men and young men; they are made in an inimitable manner, perfectly tailored, and in a large number of seasonable weaves, those that are the product of the world's best mills.

. If we desired, we could sell you cheaper clothes that might seem to be as good, and we could make a larger profit, but we cannot sell you any better, for they combine the very best in cloth, the very best in tailoring and bear the stamp of correct fashion. Can we offer you a more worthy combination? Can we better serve your demands? You may take our word for it that every suit is a perfect suit, for it bears the label that is a guarantee of its worth. Moreover, you have double assurance in buying these clothes, for not only are they vouched for by the maker, and that in no uncertain terms, but by ourselves as well. The maker is known all over the country as a pre-eminent manufacturer of the finest ready-to-wear clothes, but you can always find us at our post ready and willing to make any amends for any shortcomings, and to give you the full value of your money at all times. We look upon every sale we make as one upon which our reputation hinges. We never sold unreliable clothing—we never will.

Give us an idea of what you are looking for, and we will match it with just the model that will please you, just the goods that will suit you, and just the service that will assure you of a pleasing and profitable transaction.

THE EDSON LEWIS COMPANY
Clothiers, Hatters and Furnishers
4 and 6 Warburton Avenue
Yonkers, N. Y.